# THE HANDS OF PABLO SANTOS

Allen Sharp

## Cambridge University Press

Cambridge
London   New York   New Rochelle
Melbourne   Sydney

# Read this first

This book may be like no book that you have read before, because **you** decide the story. It is just like having an adventure in real life. What happens in the book happens to **you**. You decide what to do next and, like a real-life adventure, the end may not always be a happy one. That is up to **you**.

There are plenty of thrills and scares and you will have lots of chances to decide what you would do if you were really caught up in the adventure.

Deep in the swamps of the Florida Everglades is a wild and desolate place called Shark Slough. A place of small, tree-covered islands, surrounded by forests of twelve foot high saw grass, it is cut through by dark, narrow waterways, the home of alligators and mosquitoes.

Yet once it was the home of Calusa Indians, who lived and hunted there. Among their many tales and legends it was said that somewhere, hidden within the Slough, was the wreck of a great galleon – a pirate treasure ship.

As a child who grew up in Florida, you dreamed of finding such a treasure. That was long ago. Now, a curious note from an old friend calls you back to that world of childhood. But it is no longer a world of dreams. It has become filled with fear, mystery, murder and the supernatural. Dare you return to discover what strange fate has befallen your friend? If so, you have only to follow the simple instructions printed below.

## How to use your book

The left-hand pages of this book are numbered in the top left-hand corner. Flick the edge of your book through your fingers and you will see that the numbers are easy to find. You start reading on the page marked 1 and when you come to the end of the opposite page it will tell you where to go next. As you go through the book, there will be times when you have to make a choice about what to do next. As you come to the end of the page you will see what the choice is. You choose what you are going to do by turning to the number of the page shown in brackets beside your choice.

*Example* 'Down the stairs, I could see that the back door was open. Was there someone else in the house? Should I make a dash for that open door (**11**), or wait quietly in the darkness (**9**)?'

If you decide to make a dash for the door, then you will turn to page 11. If you decide to wait, then you will turn to page 9.

To be completely successful on your adventure you must do two things – discover what gruesome secret lies in the 'treasure' of Shark Slough, and lay to rest the strange phantom that watches over it. But remember that if you fail the first time, you can always try again. As you go through the book you may find that it is useful to refer to the map printed on the page opposite which shows all the places you may visit.

**Now turn to page 1.**

# 1

It was late on that summer's evening when I arrived in Flamingo. I'd parked my car and trailer on the site I'd reserved through the agency in Miami, and walked straight out to the Keefer place.

When I reached the small grocery store, it was closed and shuttered. I'd hardly expected it to be open at that time of night, but it looked as if it had been deserted for a long time. I took the narrow footpath down by the side of the store that led to the house at the back.

The house was well hidden by trees but, from the overgrown state of the path, I was beginning to wonder what I would find when I reached it.

The house was in a worse state than I could have guessed. Paint was peeling off. The timber was rotting and weeds grew up between the boards of the verandah. The garden was a wilderness. A strangler fig was twined about the trunk of the big oak tree. A high wind must have caught the red barked gumbo limbo by the gate and it was leaning at a crazy angle. The ground was covered with wild ferns and they had spread across what had once been the neat path up the front garden. The whole thing was steadily turning back into the natural jungle from which it had been claimed forty years before.

As I stood by what remained of the front gate, a voice said, 'It's haunted, you know.'

I turned my head to see a skinny, freckled kid standing beside me. He reminded me of someone I used to know.

'I ain't kiddin' you,' the boy went on. 'Me an' my friends, we've all seen an' heard things.'

I asked him what sort of things.

'You know,' he said, 'spooky things – flickerin' lights an' weird noises. Used to belong to a screwy guy called Keefer.'

'And what happened to him?'

'He just disappeared,' was the answer, 'but that were a few months back, before I came here. My father's got a job at the big hotel, but I knows the story. My friend Gus Willett were here when it happened.'

Turn to page 2.

# 2

The boy began telling me about a place twenty miles north of Flamingo, a desolate spot which is the home of alligators and mosquitoes. It is called Shark Slough and drains into the headwaters of the Shark River which empties into the Gulf of Mexico. The boy explained that there were once Indians living in the Slough and that amongst their tales and legends was a story of a sunken pirate treasure ship.

I already knew about both the Slough and the treasure ship. Marty Keefer, myself, and Stella Hollis had once spent most of one summer searching for it. I didn't stop him. I wanted to hear the rest of the story.

According to the boy, Marty Keefer had 'disappeared' once before, back in the winter when there was a bad drought. On that occasion, he had returned. He had been in the Slough and, so went the story, had found both the ship and the treasure. At least he had returned to Flamingo with what was said to be a gold casket full of jewels. All of that was just possible. It was the rest of the story which I found unbelievably strange.

Marty had returned, with his treasure, to the house – this house. He hadn't reopened the grocery store. In fact he hardly ever left the house. He was seen at the windows at all times of night and could be heard shouting; no-one knew at what. On the few occasions he ventured out, he looked frightened and acted as if something were following him. Then, suddenly, one morning the house was seen to be completely shuttered and Marty Keefer was gone. It was after that that the house had taken on the reputation of being 'haunted'.

'My friend, Gus Willett,' the boy told me, 'he says that somebody murdered him for the treasure. The body's still hid somewhere and it's his restless spirit that's returned to haunt the house.'

I suspected that Gus Willett read too many comic books. I saw the boy looking up at the sky.

'It's getting dark,' he said. 'This ain't a good place to be after dark. You a visitor?'

I said I was. The boy wished me a good vacation and went off down the path, whistling (3).

# 3

The house certainly did appear to be empty, but I had a good reason for making sure. I forced my way up the overgrown path to the front door. The knocker was rusted solid. I banged on the wood panels. There were no lights and no sound, other than the fading echoes of my own knocking. There was little I could do that night except return to my own trailer.

Flamingo is no ordinary town. On the map, it looks as if it's in the middle of nowhere, and in a sense, it is! It lies on the south coast of Florida. To the south is Florida Bay, filled with tiny islands which battle for survival against storm and tide. To the west are the Florida 'Capes'; desolate, hurricane swept beaches that border the waters of the Gulf of Mexico. To the north lie a hundred and fifty miles of swamp and jungle – the Everglades.

The Everglades are a National Park and Flamingo is a town that was created for tourists. Less than a hundred mile drive from Miami along a modern highway, Flamingo aims to offer all the comforts of home as well as being a place from which to visit some of the wildest parts of the 'Glades'.

To me, it was something more. With my father one of the first 'Park Rangers' who led visitors on jungle trips, I was born and grew up in the town. My two closest friends were Stella Hollis, whose father owned a gas station, and Marty Keefer, whose folks ran a grocery store.

I'd left Flamingo at the end of my college days, after my parents had both died. Stella had married a high school teacher and gone to live in Los Angeles. Only Marty remained and, when his parents died, he had taken over the grocery. It seemed a long time ago and, as with many childhood friendships, I'd lost all contact with Stella and Marty.

I was almost back at the trailer park. Nearby, a small diner was still open and I remembered that I hadn't eaten since leaving Miami. The diner smelled of burgers and fried onions. The night was still hot and sticky. I wasn't sure that I wanted a cooked meal, but if I ate there I wouldn't have to cook for myself (5). However, I supposed I could fix a light snack in my trailer (7).

# 4

When I got back to the Keefer house, it was black and silent. It didn't look like there were any 'ghosts' at work tonight. I'd brought a flashlight with me out of the car but, so far, there'd been just enough light left in the night sky to find my way without using it.

I had one idea about how I might get in. It was a long shot that it would still work, but it was worth a try. It was a trick I had learned from Marty in the days when he had arrived home late and found himself locked out.

I made my way around to the back door of the house. It was locked, as I expected. I pushed on the top corner of the door, at the same time, pulling up the handle. It still worked! I felt the bolt of the lock slip out of the door frame. The door was open. I closed it behind me before switching on the flashlight.

If I'd taken many more steps in the dark, I could well have broken my ankle. Several of the floorboards had been ripped up from the kitchen floor and stacked against one wall. Much of the rest of the ground floor was in the same state. All of the drawers and cupboards had been emptied and some of the furniture pulled apart. Somebody had been searching for something and was prepared to take the house apart, inch by inch. It didn't look like they were finished!

I made my way up the stairs. The same kind of searching had been going on there. I had been in all of the rooms, except one. I remembered it as the large bedroom on the front of the house used by Marty's parents – and probably since then by Marty himself. I opened the door.

The house was warm and sticky, like the night, but as I stepped into the room, it had an unnatural coldness about it. More than that, it had an 'atmosphere' about it – one I didn't like.

I decided to do a quick flash around with the light and get out, but then I stopped. The beam was lighting up a patch of wall covered in a faded flowered wallpaper. It was covered in more than wallpaper.

If this was the room Marty had used, then maybe the story was true and Marty Keefer was mad! (6)

# 5

The diner was still quite full, but I was grateful for the fact that it did have air-conditioning. I was pleased to find that I could order a salad and iced tea.

While I waited for it, I took an envelope from my pocket and sat having yet another look at the note which came in it.

'Folks is supposed to come to Flamingo to enjoy thereselves. You look like you got problems!'

A friendly girl was just laying my order down on the table.

'Just one problem,' I said, trying to look more cheerful. 'I've come a long way, expecting to meet an old friend. I arrive to find his house all shut up and I'm told that he's "disappeared".'

'Your friend wouldn't be that guy, Keefer?' the girl asked.

'Yes,' I answered. 'He is.'

'Yeah,' she said, 'I heard about it. Truth is, nobody weren't talkin' about nothin' else. There ain't much excitin' happens in Flamingo an' what with the treasure, an' him actin' that funny – an' then just – like vanishin' . . .'

I interrupted to ask if anyone had any ideas about where he'd gone, or what might have happened.

'Oh! Yeah!' she replied. 'There weren't no shortage on ideas. Some thinks he has gotten hisself murdered for the treasure. Some says as he's gone back to the Slough lookin' for more.'

She had to leave me at that point to see to other customers, but now I knew that the story the boy had told me wasn't just something that his friend Gus Willett had dreamed up!

The note in my hand had nothing on it but a scrawled message, 'I needs your help – desperate', and was signed, 'Marty'. If the envelope was to be believed it had been mailed in Flamingo a week before – by a man who had already 'disappeared'!

I hadn't taken the boy too seriously about the 'haunting', but was something going on in that 'empty' house? I wondered whether I should go back and do a bit of 'ghost hunting' of my own (**4**), or wait to see what I might discover in the morning after a good night's sleep (**8**).

# 6

I moved the light slowly around. There was almost no part of the walls which wasn't filled with writing and drawings, all done with felt pens, several in colour. The light stopped on something which said, 'I gotta take you back to Coco Plum!' Beneath that was, 'I don't know what you want,' and 'I ain't goin' down there again!'

If the writing was strange, the drawings were quite frightening. Most of them were of a child with big eyes and black hair. The hair hung part over the face and, in some unaccountable way, looked wet! He was dressed in some kind of long shirt, or tunic, which came down to his knees. The legs and feet had been drawn in, but there were no hands – not on any of the drawings. The arms ended with the ends of the wide sleeves and the edges had been coloured red as if they were soaked in blood!

One half of me wanted to see everything in the room. The other half wanted to get out. When I'd taken the flashlight from the seat of my car I'd also picked up my folding Polaroid camera, and slipped it into my pocket. I got it out and, using the flash, photographed every bit of the walls. I checked the prints to see that they were all sharp. The last one included the first thing that I'd read – 'I gotta take you back to Coco Plum!'

I didn't understand it, but it meant something to me. There was no such place as 'Coco Plum' – not, that is, except to three people: Marty, Stella and myself. Among the narrow waterways of Shark Slough are many small, tree-covered islands. The summer that we had visited the Slough, we had camped on one of them. Because the only trees on the island were coco plums, we called it 'Coco Plum Island'.

There was a slight creak from somewhere down the stairs. I crept quietly to the head of the stairs and looked down. There were no lights and no sound. I could see down the staircase, through the kitchen to the back door. It was standing open. I'd certainly closed it. It could have sprung open and that could have been the noise. Or was someone else now in the house?

Should I wait (**9**), or make a dash for that door (**11**)?

# 7

The diner looked pretty full as I passed it and made my way on to the trailer park. The park itself was unlit except for lights in the windows of some of the trailers. It reminded me that I had a flashlight in the car and that I should get it out.

A late arrival at the park was just swinging in off the road. As the car headlights swept around, just for a moment, they lit the light blue of my own trailer. They passed quickly on, but in that moment I saw something else! A man was standing at the door of the trailer and, unless I was very much mistaken, was trying to force the lock. I started to run.

I had covered only a few yards when the car stopped and switched off its engine. In the sudden silence I could hear hurried footsteps retreating into the distance. I ran on, but only to find what I already expected. The would-be intruder was gone, no doubt scared off by the car headlights.

I got the flashlight from the car and took a look at the door lock on the trailer. The paintwork had suffered a few scratches, but there was no real damage to either the door or the lock. I supposed that with perhaps a thousand or more visitors in Flamingo, there were bound to be one or two who weren't exactly honest.

I went back to the car to lock it up and thought that it might also be wise to remove the folding Polaroid camera that I kept on the back seat. Beside the camera, was an envelope. It contained not so much a letter as a scrawled note. That note was the reason for my being in Flamingo. All it said was, 'I needs your help – desperate!' and it was signed, 'Marty'. I put it in my pocket.

The note had been puzzling enough when it had arrived at my home in Wilmington, South Carolina, three days before. In the last hour it had become more puzzling still. The envelope in which it had come was postmarked 'Flamingo' and dated the seventeenth – only seven days ago.

Now it seemed, it had been mailed by a man who had disappeared 'a few months back'! (**8**)

**8**

I was fixing myself a pillow and a couple of sheets in the bedroom of the trailer when there was a noise from the small kitchen next door. I stuck my head around the doorway. Above the stove there was a ventilator, which was open. On the stove lay an envelope. It looked like it had just been 'mailed' through the ventilator!

I grabbed my flashlight and rushed out of the trailer. The beam cut a good distance into the darkness, but I couldn't see or hear anyone nearby. I went back inside and took the envelope into the living area where I had the best light. It contained just two photographs, Polaroid prints, probably taken with a camera like I had myself. They were both shots of parts of the walls of a room – walls covered with writing and drawings.

The prints were sharp, but too small to make out much detail. I got my camera, unscrewed the lens and used it as a magnifier. The first words I read were, 'I gotta take you back to Coco Plum!' Beneath that was, 'I don't know what you want', and 'I ain't goin' down there again!' The drawings were weird – mostly of a boy with big eyes and dark hair. He was wearing some sort of shirt which showed the lower part of his legs and feet, but there were no hands – not on any of the drawings. The ends of the sleeves had been coloured red as if they were soaked in blood!

On the edge of one print was part of a window with a garden beyond. I could see the red of a gumbo limbo tree leaning at a crazy angle by a gate. It was the Keefers' garden! And the writing on the walls must be Marty's!

Whoever had delivered the prints obviously didn't want to be seen, but why had they been delivered at all? Was this a way of inviting me to break into the Keefer house to see something for myself? The thought of going back in the dark had certainly crossed my mind (**14**). Breaking in in daylight without being seen would be no easy task.

Could the messenger have been Marty – or was Marty already dead? If the messenger was something to do with Marty's 'sudden disappearance', it might be safer to stay put in the trailer (**12**)!

# 9

I switched off my flashlight and stood, listening, in the dark. I could hear nothing, but thought it might be wise not to show my light. I'd left my camera on the floor by the doorway of Marty's room. I was sure I could find it in the dark.

I'd forgotten one thing – the missing floorboards. My foot suddenly went down six inches further than I'd expected! I hadn't hurt myself badly, but I'd made enough noise to raise the dead and the flashlight had shot out of my hand, rolled down the stairs and was probably lying broken on the kitchen floor.

The house was quiet again. It looked as if I was alone, and I wasn't risking breaking my neck on the way out. I'd seen an old-fashioned kerosene lamp in Marty's bedroom, still with some oil in it. With more care than before, I got back into the room, found the lamp and, with matches which I always carried, got it lit. I picked up my camera, turned up the lamp and went back to head of the stairs.

It was then that somebody hit me! The blow might have been aimed for my head, but it caught me across the shoulders. I grabbed the handrail of the stairs to save myself, but I lost the lamp. I saw it break, splattering flaming kerosene down the stairs as it went. A second blow sent me rolling down after it.

For a few seconds, I must have been half senseless. Then, I remember, I found myself standing up in the hallway. The staircase was ablaze from top to bottom. I turned around. The lamp must have rolled on into the kitchen. The broken floorboards were well alight and the smoke was too thick to see the back door.

If there was any other way out, I wasn't going to try the kitchen. The burning stair rails were beginning to fall, blocking the way to the front door. I tried the room to my left. It was well lit by the flames, but the fire itself hadn't yet spread that far, though the room was filling with smoke. The only way out would be through one of the windows.

I should have remembered that they were shuttered and locked on the outside (**16**)!

# 10

Jake Cuseck was one of the biggest operators on the marina and it was just possible he might even remember me from the old days. The sign, 'Jake's Jungle Jaunts', made him easy enough to find. I thought I recognised him supervising the loading of a line of tourists into boats. The line stretched a fair way along the jetty and I decided to wait.

Just below me was a ramp down to the water and, at the bottom, a mechanic was working on one of the air boats. An air boat is just a flat-bottomed boat with a big plane propellor mounted on the back. It is literally 'blown' along and is ideal for flooded swamp where the grass is not too tall. He had taken off the heavy wire mesh covers which normally protect the propellor blades and was making a lot of noise revving the engine.

The line was moving along behind me. Suddenly someone crashed into me from behind and I was thrown towards the ramp. I couldn't keep my balance. I fell and started to roll down the ramp – straight towards the blades of the spinning propellor!

I remember hearing a lot of shouting – from the

people above me – and probably some of my own! The mechanic wouldn't hear it for the noise of the engine. If I hit those blades, I would be mince-meat!

I can have been only inches away when I became conscious that the blades were turning away from me. All I hit was the water!

People came running down the ramp to help me. I wasn't really hurt – apart from being wet, bruised and very shaken. As I was helped up out of the water, I saw what had happened. At the bottom of the ramp were two iron rings. Ropes from the boat had been run through them, then fastened to bollards on the jetty, to stop the boat taking off. One of the ropes hung loose. Someone had cut it. The air boat, held only at one side, had swung round and stopped against another small boat moored beside it. The propellor had done no good to its paintwork, having just about scraped off its name – 'STELLA'!

I was now being helped up the ramp, but not before I had seen something. The name 'STELLA' had been painted over another name. I could see the letters 'DOLPH' beneath it (**13**).

# 11

I took the stairs three at a time and was out through the back door and into the wilderness of the garden. It had taken me only seconds to get out of the house, but that was long enough to glance quickly through the open doorway of a downstair room as I ran across the hall; long enough to think that I had seen someone standing back in the shadows!

I wasn't going back around the front of the house, the way I'd come. Someone could easily have let themselves out at the front and be there, waiting for me. I knew Flamingo well enough to know other ways of getting back to my trailer.

I wasn't surprised that someone was in the house. From the state of the place, they'd been there several times before. I was very certain that I'd closed the back door behind me and it stuck in my mind that as I'd taken hold of the door on my way out, I'd felt that the bolt was still sticking out in the 'locked' position. Someone had got in using the same trick as myself – and I thought that only three people could know that trick: Marty, Stella and myself!

Back at the trailer, I looked again at the photographs I'd taken, hoping that some answers might come together in my mind. That someone was searching the house, was certain – and it had to be for Marty's treasure. If Marty's 'disappearance' was because he had been murdered, what about the note in my pocket?

If Marty had been murdered he couldn't have written it, and it was a forgery. Whoever was searching the house had probably read the writing on the walls: 'I gotta take you back to Coco Plum!' They hadn't found the treasure and didn't know where Coco Plum was. They had written to me, hoping that I was going to tell them.

Something else was in my mind. If Marty had gone back to the Slough, he'd need a boat. Marty had always owned a small boat, *Stella*, named after Stella Hollis. If Marty was in the Slough, the boat should be missing.

The boat was always moored in Flamingo's marina. My first task in the morning would be to discover whether it still was (**10**).

# 12

I knew that if I went to bed, I wouldn't sleep. There was too much on my mind. If the photographs were an invitation, why wasn't there some kind of note? Someone was assuming a lot – that I would recognise Marty's writing and that I would recognise it as the Keefer House. Did they contain some different message, and was I missing it?

I looked at them again. I kept coming back to the first thing that I'd read: 'I gotta take you back to Coco Plum!' I didn't understand it, but it did mean something to me. There was no such place as 'Coco Plum' – not, that is, except to three people: Marty, Stella and myself. Among the narrow waterways of Shark Slough are many small, tree-covered islands. The summer that the three of us visited the Slough, we camped on one of them. Because the only trees on the island were coco plums, we called it 'Coco Plum Island'.

I decided that there were just two explanations of Marty's disappearance. Either Gus Willett was right – Marty had been murdered for his treasure – or he had gone back to Shark Slough. That didn't explain the note mailed in Flamingo seven days ago. I compared the writing on the photographs with the note. It looked the same, but there were small differences – like the tail on the 'y' and the way the 't' was crossed. Perhaps Marty didn't write the note. Perhaps someone did who would like to know the whereabouts of 'Coco Plum'!

If Marty was dead, I didn't think I was going to find the body. If he'd gone back to the Slough, he'd need a boat to do it. Marty always had a small boat. It was called 'Stella' after Stella Hollis. Perhaps it was not Marty I should be looking for, but Marty's boat!

I did get a few hours of broken sleep and, next morning, after breakfast, set off for Flamingo's marina. I was out of the trailer park and past the diner when I noticed a column of smoke rising up from somewhere across the town. I stopped to check my bearings. The smoke was on a line which would pass through the Keefer house. Should I go on to the marina (**10**), or first find out where the smoke was coming from (**19**)?

# 13

Waiting for me at the top of the ramp was Jake Cuseck. The fact that he spoke to me by name meant that he had remembered me. He was full of apologies, promising to have some strong words with his mechanic about testing an uncovered propellor where somebody could fall into it.

'Good job I thought to cut the rope,' he said. 'Was just lucky I even had a knife with me. Come on into the office.'

If I'd had any thoughts about someone having designs on my life, it looked as if I could cross Jake off the list of suspects. So far as I could see, he'd just saved it!

Once in the office, I didn't have to start asking questions. It was Jake who started to talk about Marty.

'I feels kinda guilty about Marty,' he told me. 'You obviously heard the story – and about the treasure. Maybe you don't know but, so far as I knows, I was the only one that ever seed it. It were when Marty come back from the Slough an' was unloadin' the boat. This sack comes untied, and out falls this gold box. The way folk tells the story now, it were a box o' jewels. I never saw no jewels. I never seed what's in the box. Marty gets it back in the sack that quick, I hardly seed the box.'

I asked him why he said that he felt guilty.

'Cause I starts the story goin' around. I don't know why Marty left Flamingo, but one reason might be as there was always sightseers hangin' around the house.'

'And you've no idea where he's gone?' I asked.

'I'd have taken a bet on it bein' the Slough,' Jake answered, 'but Marty's boat's still here, tied up where you near had that accident.'

Did Jake know it wasn't Marty's boat?

'Tell you what,' Jake suggested. 'I gotta take some supplies up to Gator Jo. Jo's no talker, but you bein' a friend of Marty's, maybe she'd talk to you.'

'Gator Jo' was an old Indian woman who lived near the Slough and sold alligator skin souvenirs to tourists. The offer was tempting (**18**), but would I be wiser to visit the Slough alone and in secret (**24**)? It might be done with the help of a local 'fixer' – a man called Mulligan.

# 14

I'd brought my flashlight but, not wanting to be seen, I'd tried not to use it. Luckily there had still been enough light in the night sky for me to find my way to the house. I made my way around to the back. Marty used to have a trick for opening the back door, even when it was locked. I was hoping that it might still work.

It was a trick that I wasn't going to need! The back door was standing open. There were no sounds and all that I could see inside was blackness. The open door suggested that those photographs were an invitation, but I still felt the need to be a little cautious. I'd been in the house many times in the past, and knew it well. The door to the hallway was right opposite the back door across the kitchen. I thought I could get that far, still without a light.

I trod very softly, and must have just about reached the doorway opposite when I seemed to step on nothing! My foot went through the floor! It felt like I'd grazed my shin, banged my knee and sprained my wrist. The wrist belonged to the hand in which I'd been holding the flashlight. I heard it smash against the wall!

One thing was sure. My presence in the house was no longer a secret! I got out some matches and struck one. I could see the reason for my accident. Quite large areas of the floorboards had been ripped up! The dying light of the match reached into the hall long enough for me to see an old-fashioned kerosene lamp standing on the hall table. There was still oil in it. One match got me there. Another got the lamp lit. I turned up the flame. Somebody had been very busy searching the house – and it looked as if they weren't finished! But it also looked as if I wasn't alone in the place.

I'd come to see that room and, from the angle of the garden on the photograph, it was upstairs on the front of the house.

It was as I got to the top of the stairs that something hit me. Maybe it was meant for my head, but it caught me across the top of the shoulders. I dropped the lamp and saw it roll down the stairs, breaking and splattering flaming kerosene as it went. The second blow sent me tumbling down after it (15)!

# 15

I may have passed out, but it couldn't have been for more than seconds. The next thing I remember was picking myself up off the floor of the hallway. The staircase was well ablaze. The lamp had rolled on into the kitchen and the broken floor was burning. I couldn't see the back door for smoke.

I tried one of the other rooms. The fire hadn't spread that far but the windows were shuttered on the outside. I picked up a heavy table and flung it at the windows. The wood of the shutters must have been half rotten. The table took glass, window frame, shutters, the lot, with it into the garden. I was quick to follow it. If anyone was still upstairs, there was no sign of them. They could well have got down the stairs past me before I came to my senses.

I could hear shouting not far off. Someone else had seen the fire. I knew Flamingo well enough to get back to the trailer by a route where I wouldn't be seen.

My T-shirt was torn and singed. I got rid of it in a swamp on the way back. Once cleaned up, my scrapes and bruises were in places I could cover up. The flashlight would probably be destroyed in the fire, but it was a kind which could be bought anywhere. I saw no point in advertising the fact that I'd ever been near the Keefer House when the fire started.

Whether someone had tried to kill me, or just knock me senseless, I didn't know. What I did know was that someone had been pulling the house apart hunting for something. It had to be Marty's treasure! Had Marty been murdered?

I couldn't get out of my head the bit of writing I'd seen on the photograph – 'I gotta take you back to Coco Plum!' Only three people knew it as a place. It was the name Marty, Stella and I had given to the island where we had camped that summer in the Slough. To anyone else it was just the name of a tree.

Marty had always had a boat, *Stella*, named after Stella Hollis. If Marty had gone back to the Slough, the boat should also be missing.

If the boat was still in Flamingo, I should find it moored in the marina (**17**), or was my first job in the morning to go back and see what remained of the Keefer house after the fire (**19**)?

# 16

There was a heavy table standing in the centre of the room. It took all of my strength to lift it. I raised it as high as I could and ran with it at one of the windows.

I turned my head against the glass which would certainly fly. I heard the window break and then the splintering of wood. The house must have been more rotten than it looked. The table was now half into the garden. It had taken with it glass, window frame, shutters – the lot. I lost no time in following the table.

Once clear of the house, I stopped to look back. There was no sign of anyone still trapped upstairs. For all I knew, whoever had hit me had followed me down the stairs, passed me, and got out of the house while I was still half senseless.

Suddenly, I heard shouting nearby. Someone else had seen the fire and would soon be on the scene. I knew Flamingo well enough to find another way back to my trailer – by a route where I wouldn't be seen.

My T-shirt was torn and singed. I got rid of it in a swamp on the way back. Once cleaned up, my scrapes and bruises were in places that I could cover up. The flashlight would probably be destroyed in the fire, but it was a kind that could be bought anywhere. I saw no point in letting people know that I had been in the Keefer house when the fire had started.

Whether someone had tried to kill me, or just to knock me senseless, I didn't know. What I did know was that someone had been pulling the house apart hunting for something. It had to be Marty's treasure.

I was no nearer to knowing what had happened to Marty – maybe he had been murdered. But that line on the wall was still stuck in my mind – 'I gotta take you back to Coco Plum!' If Marty had gone back to the Slough, he'd need a boat. Marty had always had a boat, *Stella*, named after Stella Hollis. Was the boat missing as well as Marty?

If the boat was still in Flamingo, I should find it moored in the marina (**17**), or was my first job in the morning to see what remained of Marty's house (**19**)?

# 17

Jake Cuseck was one of the biggest operators on the marina, and it was just possible that he might remember me from the old days. The sign, 'Jake's Jungle Jaunts', made his place easy enough to find.

When I got there, I could see that something unusual was going on. There was a crowd of tourists standing around the building that served as the booking office and, from the raised voices, some of them didn't sound too happy. One of them was moving away from the crowd towards me. I stopped her to ask what was wrong.

'What's wrong,' she said, 'is I ain't gettin' my trip what's been booked for three days. I don' know what's goin' on. Man at the office won't say no more than all the trips is cancelled – and there's a couple o' wild rumours goin' about.'

She pointed to a cloud of smoke visible in the distance.

'Was a fire there last night – house and grocery store. They say as the body of the man who runs this place been found in the ashes. Other story is that it weren't the fire as killed him. Somebody done that with a bullet.'

She went off muttering, 'Fat chance of gettin' booked on one of they other trips today.'

I slipped past the crowd at the office to where the small boats were moored. I found one with the name Stella. It looked like Marty's boat. It also had a patch of fresh paint under the name, as if some different name had been painted out. Did somebody know that Marty had gone to the Slough and want it to look like he hadn't? Maybe Jake Cuseck knew the answer to that, but it didn't sound as if Jake would be answering any more questions!

I had to go to Shark Slough. But if Jake had been shot in the Keefer house, it could have been by someone who had decided to thin down the possible treasure seekers – with a gun! If I was going to the Slough then I had to do it quietly!

I knew just two ways of doing that. Nobody had ever tried it, but it should be possible to get into the Slough by the 'back door', from a place called Long Pine Key (**22**). The other way needed the help of a local 'fixer' – Willie Mulligan (**24**)!

# 18

I met Jake Cuseck again quite late in the afternoon. I thought that we weren't giving ourselves too much time, but Jake assured me that we would be there and back before dark and with time to spare for me to talk to Jo.

The boat was a fibreglass job with oars and a small outboard motor. The outboard would be useful for getting us quickly through Whitewater Bay so that we needed to row for less than half the twenty-five mile journey.

'Would have set out sooner,' Jake said, 'but I been listenin' to the newscasts – see what's been happenin' to hurricane "Daisy".'

I told him I didn't know there was a hurricane warning out.

'There ain't,' Jake replied. 'Daisy's been on her way up from the Caribbean these last forty-eight hours. She's still headed north up the Gulf of Mexico. It's fair certain we ain't goin' to see her.'

I hoped he was right!

We reached Whitewater Bay and started running on the outboard. Jake had been watching a rare sight in Whitewater, a manatee, half a ton of

Florida sea cow, with two pups, its strange wrinkled and whiskered face constantly popping out of the water near the boat. But something else caught my attention. Over to the west was the great wall of mangroves that separated us from the coast. The tops of the trees were filled with cormorants. Cormorants are usually constantly on the move, but these birds were just sitting. I looked at the sky beyond. A bank of dark cloud was building up above the horizon.

As we neared the end of the bay and turned between the maze of islands that mark the mouth of the Shark River I noticed that the sky was beginning to fill with birds – heron, pelican, darters and water turkey – all flying east. I pointed it out to Jake but he dismissed it as the normal evening flights of the birds.

We used the outboard for as long as we could until it was in danger of tangling with the plants in the now shallower water. Jake switched off the engine. There was a sudden silence, a silence in which even the chorus of frogs and insects was missing (**23**).

# 19

What had yesterday been a house and a grocery store was now not much more than a heap of still smouldering ashes. That was as much as I could see of the Keefer place from behind the barrier which the Flamingo Fire Department had set up around it. I stood outside the gas station fifty yards down the road – the same gas station once owned by Stella Hollis's father until he was bought out by Rufus Pratt. Rufus was coming out of the station towards me.

'I remembers you!' he said. 'Used to see you with Stella Hollis afore I buys this place off of her old man.'

'That's right,' I replied. 'I'm visiting – just got in last night.'

'Gee! I'm sorry!' Rufus exclaimed. 'I'm forgettin' as you was a friend of Marty's. Bad business!'

'You mean the mystery of Marty's disappearance,' I said. 'Yes, I heard the story last night.'

'Yuh don't know, does you!' Rufus said. 'It ain't no mystery no more.' He looked towards where I could see a Sheriff's Deputy talking to two of the firemen. 'They found Marty's body in them ashes.'

Before I could say anything, the Deputy came across to speak to Rufus.

'Reckon you were lucky last night that there weren't no wind. Can't let you open up for a while yet, not while them ashes is still hot. Maybe later today.'

He looked as if he was moving off; then he stopped and turned back.

'Thought I'd tell you,' he said. 'That body. It's not Keefer – leastwise not accordin' to the "dog tag" on the wrist. It's Jake Cuseck. He didn't die in the fire neither. We'll have to wait for the medical examiner, but I thinks I knows the kinda hole a .32 slug makes in a skull when I sees one.'

Rufus Pratt's jaw dropped open. When he closed it, he managed to say, 'Glad I ain't no bettin' man! Bein' as Jake were the only one as saw Marty's gold box, if it were anyone done for Marty, I'd have staked on it bein' Jake Cuseck. Reckon an apology's goin' ter be kinda difficult!'

**(20)**

# 20

'Poor Jake!' Rufus went on, shaking his head slowly from side to side. 'I sees him just yesterday – or maybe it were the day afore. Comes in to fill the car up with gas. We was talking about fishin'. Jake was sayin' as the best fishin' he'd done was some long time since – an' he couldn't for the life of him remember the place. Only name in his mind was some island there. Thought it might have bin called Coco Plum Island. But I ain't never heard of the place.'

So Jake Cuseck had been 'fishing' – fishing around for the whereabouts of Coco Plum Island. I wondered whether it was because he thought Marty was there, or because he thought Marty's treasure was there. Jake certainly wasn't going to be telling me. There was only one way I was going to find out – and that was by going to Shark Slough.

In the last few minutes, things had become a lot more difficult. I wondered if anyone was going to find out that I'd been at the Keefer house last night. I didn't want to become caught up in a murder investigation.

That wasn't the only thing that worried me. I was asking myself why Jake had been shot. Jake was supposed to be the only one to have seen Marty's treasure. Jake was also one of the big boat operators in Flamingo. He could know if Marty had gone back to the Slough. Had he perhaps found the treasure, or was someone else looking, someone who had decided to thin down the competition – with a gun!

The sooner I left Flamingo and went to the Slough, the better. But if there was a killer around, I was going to have to do it quietly!

I knew of two ways of doing that. There was a kind of 'back door' to the Slough which could be reached from a place called Long Pine Key. I knew of no-one who'd ever tried it, but it should be just possible (**22**).

My other choice was a different kind of risk. It meant my enlisting the help of Flamingo's biggest 'fixer'–Willie Mulligan – a man who would arrange anything for the right price (**24**)!

# 21

I walked around the trailer. The ventilator over the stove, which I always kept open, was closed. I used the metal key which was for turning on the gas bottles to smash one of the trailer windows. The smell confirmed what I suspected. It was full of gas. I gave it plenty of time to clear before opening the trailer door.

On the edge of the door was a beautifully simple device. The striking surface from a matchbox had been folded over the heads of two matches and was held in place by a strong rubber band. The match sticks were glued to the door and the striking surface to the door frame. When the door was opened, the matches were pulled out, so lighting them. If the trailer had still been full of gas, there wouldn't have been much left to show how the explosion had happened!

I didn't think I could affort to wait around in Flamingo until morning, and I couldn't be certain that what had happened had nothing to do with Willie Mulligan! I telephoned an old business friend in Miami who owed me several favours. I wasn't giving him much time, but he promised to do what I asked. I spent the afternoon shopping for supplies and camping equipment and, at four o'clock, I left Flamingo.

Fifteen miles along the highway to Miami, I turned off onto the loop road to the place called Long Pine Key. I stopped five miles short of it and drove the car and trailer off the road and into the trees.

A fifty-yard walk brought me to the edge of the swamp. Not far across the water I could see the wall of twelve foot high saw grass that marked the 'back door' to Shark Slough. Beside me, half hidden in the undergrowth was what my friend had had delivered for me from Miami, probably no more than an hour before – a boat.

Stuck to the boat was an envelope with a message in it: 'Don't know where you're going, but good luck! Suggest you check on newscast before you leave.' I wanted to get moving to find Coco Plum Island before dark (**25**). The note didn't say why I should listen to the newscast. Did I have time to sit listening to the car radio to find out (**27**)?

# 22

I telephoned an old business friend in Miami. I'd done him a few favours in my time and he 'owed' me. I told him exactly what I wanted. Apart from telling me I must be mad and complaining that I wasn't giving him very much time, he promised to make the arrangements.

Long Pine Key is actually an island. 'Key' in Florida is just another name for an island. Long Pine happens to be an island in the middle of a swamp. Formed by a ridge of limestone and covered by slash pines, it's a favourite spot with fishermen as well as tourists in general. Nothing like as big as Flamingo, it too has its camping sites and boat trips.

I needed to buy myself some supplies and some pieces of camping equipment. By the time I had done that, it was getting towards the end of the afternoon before I drove out of Flamingo.

About fifteen miles out of the town, I left the main highway back to Miami and turned onto the loop road which goes to Long Pine Key. About six miles short of it, I slowed down almost to walking pace. I was looking for an opening in the trees to my left. I spotted it, made certain that there was no-one else on the road to see me, and swung the car and trailer off the road and into the trees. I stopped them in a place where there was very little chance of anyone finding them.

Fifty yards' walk brought me to the edge of the swamp. Not far off across the water, I could see the wall of twelve foot high saw grass that marked the edge of Shark Slough. Half hidden in the undergrowth beside me was what my friend in Miami had had delivered earlier that afternoon – a boat.

Five miles down the road, I could have easily hired a boat at Long Pine Key. The problem was that I had no idea how long I would be in the Slough. If I'd hired a boat and failed to return the same day, I'd have had a search party out after me!

There was an envelope stuck to the boat with a note from my friend. It said, 'Don't know where you're going, but good luck! Suggest you check on newscast before you leave.' I wanted to find Coco Plum Island before dark (**25**). Had I time to sit in the car waiting for the newscasts – and about what (**27**)?

# 23

There was an unnatural stillness about the air. I looked behind us, down river to the west. The bank of black cloud that I had seen in the bay was moving swiftly towards us with sheets of rain already visible beneath it.

First the wind hit us, and then the rain. The wind outdid the slow current of the river and our boat started to be driven upstream. The water began to rise in the torrential downpour, quickly spreading beyond the river banks and into the tall mangrove trees on either side.

Jake started the outboard again. The only place where we might find some kind of shelter was Tarpon Bay, almost an inland lake which fed the headwaters of the river.

The sky was now as black as night, broken only by the jagged lightning flash. It was in such a flash that, looking back, I saw a solid wall of water moving up river towards us. It must have been all of ten feet high! I shouted to Jake. He couldn't hear me above the storm. I pulled him around by the shoulder and pointed. He began to shout back at me. Most of the words were lost in the wind, but I thought he was telling me that with the load we were carrying, if the boat were swamped, it would sink. He pointed to the trunk of a large mangrove which was floating in the water, almost alongside us. Suddenly he stood up in the boat and made a leap for the trunk. He was half on the trunk and half in the water. He pulled himself up, straddling the tree with his legs. Then he waved at me to follow.

I looked back again. The wall of water was only yards away and would strike at any second. I turned back towards Jake. The tree had drifted further from the boat. Jake was still shouting and waving me on.

Should I jump (**31**)? If I missed and the water hit me while I was somewhere between the tree and the boat, then I saw no chance of surviving. Should I stay in the boat (**26**)? Jake could be wrong about it sinking. If he was right, then I would go under with it!

# 24

Willie Mulligan was Flamingo's 'Mr Fix-it'. He'd once been a boat operator, though his boats had always enjoyed the reputation of being the second most dangerous thing in Florida Bay. The first place went to the Great White Shark! It was after losing three boats and four tourists that Willie lost his licence. Since then, Willie seemed to have found other ways of making money. It had been rumoured that he'd been questioned by the FBI about the appearance of South American cocaine in Florida. But it was probable he made his money by doing jobs on the quiet – jobs that weren't exactly legal.

What I wanted was perfectly legal. All I wanted was that it should be done quietly. I wanted a boat, some supplies and some camping equipment – and I wanted them secretly delivered to a spot in Whitewater Bay, about four miles north of Flamingo.

There I would pick them up and make my way to the Slough with little risk of anyone following me or starting to search for me if I was gone for a few days.

Willie Mulligan saw no difficulties in making those arrangements. He even 'happened' to have a boat! It was an old ex-army inflatable with almost more patches on it than boat! Willie wasn't without his touch of 'blarney'.

'One great advantage of this kind of boat,' he said, 'is that you can be repairin' it yourself with no more difficulty than a pedal cycle – and I'll be throwin' in a repair outfit entirely for free.'

For what he was going to charge me, he could afford to be that generous! Everything would be waiting for me at Whitewater in the morning.

I spent the rest of the morning in the town before going back to the trailer. My stove and refrigerator ran on bottled gas. The gas bottles were stored in a separate, ventilated compartment at the back of the trailer. As I passed the back I remembered that one was almost empty and that I should be switching over to the other. I opened up the compartment, only to find that someone had already switched over the bottles for me (**21**)!

# 25

By the time I had packed all of my supplies and equipment into the boat, a lot of clouds had gathered in the evening sky. From beneath them, a great fan of sunbeams had turned the water of the swamp to a rich gold, the blue plumage of a flock of feeding herons looking almost black against the bright water.

As I rowed out towards the Slough, they rose noisily into the air above me and circled overhead. I was nearing the wall of saw grass and began looking for entrances to the narrow, mangrove-lined waterways which would lead me into the heart of the Slough itself. At the edge of the Slough there were mounds of mud and saw grass – alligator nests, some long since abandoned and being taken over by young willows. There was a movement beside one of them and I saw a large alligator slide over the mound and vanish into one of the waterways. Since it is the alligators who keep the waterways free by gnawing through the mangrove roots, I decided to follow. A creature that size needed a lot of water to swim in – enough, I hoped for my small boat!

It looked as if I had chosen well. Only rarely did

I have to use the mangrove roots to push the boat along. Most of the time, I was able to use the oars. The sky was darkening more rapidly than I expected, but Coco Plum Island couldn't be more than two miles further on. If I could keep up my progress I'd make it before dark. It was then I noticed something. The 'ick – ick' of the grasshopper frog and the deeper throated 'urrrh' of its bigger bullfrog cousin had stopped. The familiar evening chorus was suddenly silent.

A distant rustling began in the saw grass, getting nearer as the air began to fill with birds – kites, water turkey and the large outline of brown and white pelican. More and more birds were joining the flocks and all flying swiftly east.

The birds were gone. The silence was back and the air had about it an unnatural stillness. I looked up at the sky. A wall of swirling black cloud was appearing over the grass. The howling wind and torrential rain reached me seconds later. I knew why my friend had suggested I listen to the newscast. A hurricane was on its way and now I was in it (**28**)!

# 26

The heaviest thing on the boat was the outboard motor. I had just heaved it over the side when the water struck, half filling the boat and throwing me into its bottom. I struggled to my knees. The boat had not gone under but was riding the crest of the water as it surged forward.

The lightning was still flashing, but now against a background of constant flickering light. I could see the tops of trees on either side as I sped past them at frightening speed. The water around me was jammed with floating logs and broken branches. Nowhere could I see Jake Cuseck.

Suddenly, the trees seemed to retreat on either side of me. The boat had reached Tarpon Bay. As the tidal wave which had carried me there spread out in the bay, the water level began to fall, but still I was carried forward.

Now I could see the great curtain of saw grass marking the edge of Shark Slough. The water was building up again as it was squeezed towards the narrow gaps of waterways leading to the heart of the Slough itself. As the boat rose almost to the top of the grass I could see it torn by the wind into patterns like the waves of the sea, and rising from it a black shape – huge, shuddering, its rain lashed timbers glistening in the lightning flashes. It was the stern of a great ship!

The boat plunged down. A branch must have caught me across the head and I remembered no more.

I was lying on wet ground. I tried to move. The pain in my leg told me that it was almost certainly broken. I realised that the boat was on top of me and that the light spilling in around its edges must be the first light of dawn. Gritting my teeth against the pain, I began to pull myself, ever so slowly, out from beneath the boat. Each time the pain got too bad, I rested and then tried again. It seemed like an eternity before I was free.

At last I lay in the open air. I was lying on my side and put out my hand to see if I could lift myself. I felt my hand touch another. I thought of Jake Cuseck, but the hand was cold and the flesh curiously soft to my touch (**29**).

# 27

Radio reception didn't seem to be that good in the spot where I'd parked the car. I assumed that whatever it was I was supposed to be listening for was something local and I should be tuning in to a local radio station like Miami. I played around with the tuner, getting music, commercials, sports reports – and was on the point of giving up when a voice broke in over music to say, 'We interrupt your programme to bring you the latest update on hurricane "Daisy" straight from the Florida Storm Warning Center.'

It was the first that I'd heard of hurricane Daisy which had been travelling up through the Caribbean and into the Gulf of Mexico for the past forty-eight hours. In the last two hours it had started swinging east and looked like hitting the Florida coast north of the Capes. If it kept on that track it would come right across Shark Slough!

The Slough was not a good place to be at any time. It was no place to be in the middle of a hurricane. I got out all of the rope that I had and used it to stake down the trailer. The boat, I stowed under the trailer. If trees started falling, then the car roof was stronger than the trailer. All I could do was sit it out and keep listening to the radio.

'Daisy' arrived two hours later. Without the radio, I would have known she was coming. For a half hour before, there'd been a steady flight of birds eastward. The evening sky was black with heron, spoonbills, kites, water turkey, and more pelican than I'd ever seen together in flight before. Minutes before the storm, the evening chorus of frogs and insects had suddenly died and the air had become unnaturally still.

Now the rain was lashing down and the trees bending in the howling wind. Though I'd turned it head on to the wind, the car rocked uncomfortably while branches rattled down onto it. In a sudden flash of lightning I could see what looked like half a tree lying across the car hood right in front of the windshield.

It was two more hours before the storm began to ease and I dared try snatching a few hours of sleep (**30**).

# 28

The water had begun to rise in the narrow channel. A pair of alligators surfaced in front of me and, with tails thrashing, dived beneath the boat, almost capsizing it. The boat was now being tossed along, one moment driven into the bending branches of the trees, the next, torn out by the current, spinning, rolling, colliding with broken branches strewn on the water's surface. I'd lost the oars. All I could do was crouch down in the boat, protecting my head as best I could from flying timber.

Suddenly, I felt the boat rising. I had reached a junction where three or four waterways met and emptied into one. The water was building up, lifting the boat almost to the level of the tree tops. The darkness was split apart by brilliant flashes of lightning. I could see the top of the saw grass torn by the wind into patterns like waves of the sea – and rising through it something huge and black! Shuddering, rain lashed, its timbers gleaming in the lightning-torn sky, was the stern of a great galleon!

A thunderous roar surged above the shriek of the storm. I was thrown forward in the boat.

Whatever had been holding back the water had broken. I caught a last glimpse of the great ship as it sank back into the sea of grass and the boat shot forward, carried helplessly on a tumbling wall of churning foam.

I was lying on wet ground with the boat on top of me. One of my legs, I was sure, was broken. Above me, the storm raged on. Several times I must have passed out, but I remember opening my eyes to realise that all was quiet and that the light spilling under the edges of the boat must be the light of dawn. The pain in my leg hit me the moment that I tried to move, but I had to get out. I found I couldn't lift the boat; probably because of fallen branches on top of it. There was just enough space to wriggle out. I gritted my teeth and began to move.

It seemed an eternity before I was free. I turned to ease the pain in my leg and felt my hand resting on another – a cold hand, the flesh of which gave and crumbled beneath my touch (**29**)!

# 29

The body which lay beside me was no victim of the hurricane. The rotting flesh had long been lying under water. The lips were gone, but the three gold teeth which flashed from the grinning jaw, told me that I had found Marty Keefer.

I pulled myself away from the corpse and found that I was looking from the trees into a clearing beyond. It was a clearing littered with the black timbers of a broken ship, but a clearing that I still recognised. This was Coco Plum Island!

The clearing was not empty. A man was standing, not a hundred yards away, his back to me and bending down over the wreckage. He stood up and turned. I had never seen him before but, in his hands, he was holding a gold box. Something told me that I should not shout for help. I lay there while the man vanished into the trees.

The man did not return. I made myself a rough splint from the wood that lay around. It took me six hours to cover the five miles to the head of the Shark River. That evening I was picked up by the boats returning from a jungle trip to Everglades City.

The gold box was never heard of again and the mystery surrounding it and Marty Keefer has never been solved. Only one strange fact must be added.

At about the time I was being picked up by boat at Shark River, a man was leaving Flamingo by car on the road back to Miami. Five miles out of Flamingo, the car ran into a tree, caught fire, and the driver was burned almost beyond recognition. He was never identified but, from what could be judged of his original appearance, it would have fitted exactly with the man who I saw on Coco Plum, carrying the gold box. That was not all.

The accident was witnessed by a man and wife, on the road at the time, and driving in the opposite direction. Both were prepared to swear that the accident was caused by the sudden appearance in front of the car, of a boy. They described him as having big, dark eyes and black hair. He was wearing a sort of long shirt which came down to his knees. Perhaps the shirt sleeves were just very long, but the boy appeared to have no hands!

# 30

The day dawned peacefully with the blue plumed heron back, quietly wading and feeding in the swamp. But 'Daisy' had not passed without leaving her mark. My car and trailer looked as if they had been in a major collision. There was part of a tree to remove before I could even attempt to get them out – but that worry could wait. The boat and its supplies were unharmed.

I lost no time in getting the boat loaded up and setting off for the Slough. The narrow mangrove-lined waterways were filled with floating debris from the storm, but the water level was high, taking it above the spreading mangrove roots that would normally make rowing difficult.

The journey was promising to be easier than I expected until I met a large alligator swimming towards me. Alligators are usually shy of people and will keep clear of them unless cornered or provoked. This one showed no sign of giving way. Perhaps still nervous and aggressive after the storm, it had begun to ram the boat with its snout. I had to give it two hard cracks with an oar before, with a loud, cow-like roar and a final lash of its tail, all fifteen feet of it dived beneath the boat and was gone.

It was half a mile ahead that I hit real trouble – a wide area of flattened saw grass completely blocking the waterway. It was firm enough to walk on. I reached the other side to find that it had reduced the flow of water to a mere trickle. I went back, pulled the boat up onto the grass, loaded what I could onto my back, and started walking.

There were places where I could use the sprawling mangrove roots like the rungs of a ladder. The rest of the time I was walking in wet mud – and giving a wide berth to any 'gator holes' I spotted in the banks.

In a little more than a mile I reached the edge of Coco Plum Island. I was beginning to feel exhausted and stopped to catch my breath before making my way to what I hoped was still a clearing in the centre where I could camp.

Fifty yards off, sticking out through a wall of grass, was something black. It was not a tree. It was a broken ship's mast (**32**)!

# 31

I jumped. I felt Jake's hand grab me and help me scramble onto the trunk. Almost instantly we rose feet into the air. I could see tree branches in front of us and almost level with the water. I flattened myself on the trunk, clinging desperately with knees and arms. There was a cracking of timber. The trunk swerved, hesitated and went on. I raised my head. The trunk in front of me was empty. Jake Cuseck had gone! I looked back, but there was nothing but swirling water.

The tree sped on. I had never believed the story of a great ship in the Slough was possible, but in a storm such as this, the biggest wooden ship could have been carried up the river.

I raised my head again. The trees no longer surrounded me. I had reached Tarpon Bay. In this more open area, the water level was beginning to fall. The trunk to which I clung was caught in a swirl of water, flung towards the edge of the Bay and lodged itself firmly between the trunks of two tall, close growing mangroves.

The tree remained firm while the water below me continued to fall. The storm raged on but with slowly decreasing fury. Within an hour, there was dry land below me and I climbed down to find what shelter I could from the wind and still driving rain.

With the first light of dawn, the storm was gone. Not far off, I could see the tall, storm-torn grass which marked the edge of Shark Slough. I saw that much of the floating debris had gathered around the entrance to one of the waterways leading into the Slough itself. I could not believe that Jake was still alive but, just in case, I felt I should explore the place where the water might have carried him.

I waded through the mud of the narrow waterway, sometimes able to use the sprawling mangrove roots to walk along like the rungs of a ladder, but the going was hard. Eventually I realised that I had reached one of the tree-covered islands.

I was sure it was 'Coco Plum'! It was while I was staring at it that I noticed something black sticking out of the saw grass. It was the broken mast of a ship (32)!

# 32

I forced my way between the tough, saw-edged grass. In front of me was a water-filled 'sink hole'; a deep, natural hole in the limestone rock. Just showing above the surface were the jagged timbers of the stern of a once great ship. She was lying, nearly upended, her mizzen mast horizontal and almost clear of the water.

I tried my weight on the mast. It seemed firm. I crawled along it, out over the water. Where the sun had not dried it, it was still slimy and I felt my knees begin to slide. Wildly, I grasped at the slippery wood with my hands, but next moment I was in the water!

I surfaced, filled my lungs with air, and dived. The rails of the quarter deck lay on either side with the poop deck above. What had been the bulkhead of the captain's quarters was littered with broken spars and rusted cannon. But what I had already seen in my first accidental ducking, was an open doorway to the cabin beyond.

The cabin was dimly lit from the doorway above. Only the large table at its centre remained fixed to the deck. Everything else had sunk to the farther end. Still seated in a heavy chair, was a crumbling skeleton. A second lay nearby, though still with tatters of clothing on it and a bracelet of alligator teeth about one wrist. Next to it was a gold box! I started to swim down towards it.

My movements were disturbing the water and something began to float towards me out of the deeper shadow. It was a third body – but not a skeleton. Bloated flesh still clung in places to the bones. The lips were gone and in the grinning jaws was the glint of three gold teeth. I had found Marty Keefer!

Suddenly in my mind, I was seeing the walls of that room in the Keefer house. 'I ain't goin' down there again!' 'I gotta take you back to Coco Plum!' I could feel that my breath would not last out much longer. The gold box was not huge. I thought that I could carry it back to the surface.

Should I take it with me (**34**), or should I leave it – because this was what Marty Keefer had to 'take back' and had lost his life doing (**36**)?

# 33

I dropped to the ground on the opposite side of the mast to where the man was standing.

'Don't go away!' he said, climbing over the mast to face me. 'You've got something that belongs to me.'

He clearly meant the box!

'You found it almost by accident,' he went on. 'I've done a lot of work to get here.'

'You mean like sending me forged notes from Marty Keefer,' I replied.

'Wrong!' was the answer. 'Jake Cuseck sent you the note. He wanted to know where Coco Plum Island was. I already knew, just as I know that the name of what's left of the ship down there is the *Isabella*.'

I must have looked slightly astonished.

'It's quite simple,' he said. 'I have always been interested in the pirate Jean Lafitte. In August 1788, one of Lafitte's ships, the *Isabella*, was anchored at Cozumel, an island off the Mexican coast. While she was there, her crew made some profitable raids on the coast. It seems they did particularly well in collecting the treasures of a Catholic Mission at a place called Carmilla. On August 24th the *Isabella* sailed for New Orleans. On August 26th she disappeared during a hurricane. It is about a year later that you will find the first account of Indians sighting a "great ship" in Shark Slough. I should have thought there was a good deal more treasure down there, but that box and its contents should make me quite wealthy.'

It was clear that he was going to have the box if he had to take it at gun point. I was curious about one thing, so I asked. How did he know about Coco Plum Island?

'Three people knew about Coco Plum,' he said, 'and one of them is my wife – but don't worry. She'll never hear about your unfortunate end.'

He raised the gun.

The mast behind him had started to move. If it were suddenly to whip forward, it would easily kill him! Did he really intend to shoot me in cold blood? Should I warn him (**35**), or let fate take its course (**37**)?

# 34

I picked up the box. It was heavy, even under water. It would have been easy to pull it to the surface on a rope, but I had some doubts about how far I could swim with it.

A sudden and violent shudder ran through the ship. It lasted only moments, but I was beginning to wonder how deep the hole was in which she was lying, whether the ship might sink deeper – or even begin to break up. I had no idea what sort of pounding she had taken in the hurricane of the night before. If she was breaking up, this might be the only chance to get the box out.

Looking up, I saw that I could reach the table fixed to the centre of the cabin floor. With the box tucked under my arm, and using the table's edge to pull myself up, I scrambled onto its top edge. Now, by flexing my legs, I could push myself up far enough to grasp the cabin doorway and haul myself onto the other side of the bulkhead.

I was still only half way to the surface. Having spent a childhood diving for lobsters, I could hold my breath underwater for almost as long as the legendary Japanese pearl divers but, already, I was feeling the effects of the extra effort on my lungs.

I had decided to leave the box, go up to the surface for air and dive again, when the ship started to move once more. I saw one of the big iron cannon rolling over the rubble on the bulkhead towards me. Before it reached me, it had gone down through the cabin doorway and I could hear the smashing of timber below.

I struggled to the edge of the quarter deck, siezed the rail and begin to haul myself up. Every foot of the way, I felt more sure that I couldn't make it, when my head, dizzy through lack of air, finally broke the surface. Slowly, it cleared, as I gulped huge mouthfuls of air into my aching chest.

I swam the few yards to the mast, pushed the box onto it and clambered after it. Remembering how I had got into the water, this time, I straddled the mast with my legs, put the box in front of me and inched my way slowly towards dry land (38).

# 35

I shouted to the man to look out behind him; that the mast was moving. He hesitated, not knowing whether to believe me. Then he half turned. It was too late! The mast swung up in a great arc, flinging him high in the air. I saw him splash down into the centre of the pool. The mast was now upright in the water and visibly sinking.

I waited for a few seconds, but he didn't reappear. The mast was gone and the water lay still and empty. I dived into the pool and swam down to where I had seen him enter the water. There was nothing – no trace of the man or the ship. I tried a second time before hauling myself out onto the edge. I was alone again and with the gold box by my feet.

I bent down to look at it more closely. It clearly had a lid, but I could see no kind of lock. I pulled on the lid and, suddenly, it came open.

The box was not solid gold. Thin sheets of the beaten metal were laid over the surface of some kind of dark wood. Its weight came from a thick lining of lead. The box was not empty. In it lay two shrivelled hands, cut off at the wrists. They were very small, like the hands of a child.

In my mind, I was again seeing the pictures on the walls of the room in the Keefer house, those strange, almost frightening drawings of a child – a child with no hands! What did it mean? Marty had seen those same hands that were now in front of me. Were the drawings of something he had dreamt up in his imagination, or were they drawings of something which he had actually seen!

I was feeling more and more uneasy. That Marty was dead was certain, but how had he died? Marty Keefer was a better swimmer and diver than myself. I was remembering the moment in that cabin when I had decided not to take the box, only to find that I could no longer escape. Yet when I had picked up the box, my escape had been made suddenly easy.

Had Marty died because the hands had prevented him from leaving without them? The thought was too ridiculous, yet the uncertainty in my mind remained.

The box was not valuable. I could push it back into the pool (**40**). But I was curious to find out more about those hands – should I take it with me (**42**)?

# 36

I had not come looking for treasure. I had come looking for Marty Keefer. Now, I had found him and there was no longer any way in which I could help him – except, perhaps, by respecting his last wishes.

I turned in the water and began to swim up to the cabin doorway above me. As I neared it, the ship gave a sudden lurch. It settled down again quickly, but the movement had shifted some loose spars. They now lay across the doorway, blocking my escape!

I tried to move them. There were still small gaps through which I could see. I thrust my arm through one of them, feeling about with my hands to find what was holding the timbers so firmly. My fingers touched cold metal. One of the heavy iron cannon was lying on top of the spars!

I couldn't hope to move the cannon. If I could break the timbers around it, I might still escape. I needed something heavy – the gold box! I dived again. The box was heavy, even underwater. As a child, I had dived for lobsters and could hold my breath for almost as long as the legendary

Japanese pearl divers, but I knew how fast the extra effort would be using up the air in my lungs. I hauled myself up onto the table fixed to the cabin's deck. Holding the box above my head, I could get enough push with my legs to propel myself at the doorway.

It must have been at the instant that I reached it that the ship moved again. I heard the cannon roll away as I shot through the loose timber and up towards the surface. I used the last of my air and the last of my strength to keep on kicking out with my legs. I was near to blacking out, when my head broke the surface.

The mast was just above me. I held it while I gulped mouthfuls of fresh air. Eventually, I contrived to get both myself and the box onto the mast. Remembering what had happened before, I straddled the mast with my legs, pushing the box in front of me.

What I had not seen was the man standing on the bank waiting for me – a stranger – a stranger holding a rifle (**33**)!

# 37

The mast, which had been moving only slowly, now sprang forward, at the same time whipping upwards through the air in a great arc. The man was swept off his feet and tossed out over the water. He vanished with a loud splash. The mast was now standing upright in the centre of the pool and, as I watched, began to sink beneath the water.

I watched for the man to reappear. He did not. I dived, swimming down to below where I had seen him enter the water. I could see nothing. I came up for air and tried a second time. Both man and ship were gone. The water lay still and empty.

I climbed out and turned to pick up the box. As yet I did not even know what it contained. I could not see it! The box had gone!

My first thought was that the man had got out of the water while I was searching for him and had taken the box away. I made my way back through the saw grass to the place where I had first entered it. The man must have been planning to camp, for I now saw his gear lying near the edge of the island. If he had taken the box, then he would certainly have taken at least part of his gear with him – like his water canteen and something in which to carry the box.

Beside my foot, there was a part bare footprint in the mud. There was only one person who walked these swamps barefoot – Gator Jo, the old Indian woman who lived near Tarpon Bay. This was her hunting ground for the alligators whose skins ended up as purses and wallets for the tourists.

I'd known Jo since I was a child and had remembered a few of the lessons she had taught me. I made my way onto the island and climbed one of the tallest trees. There was no way that you could move around the Slough without disturbing the thousands of birds who lived there. From my treetop vantage point, I watched a succession of them flying up from amongst the saw grass. Whoever was moving through the grass was moving swiftly and surely. It was a zig-zag path, but the direction was obvious – towards Jo's cabin on Tarpon Bay. I climbed down the tree and, though with considerably less certainty and skill, headed in the same direction (**45**).

# 38

I was hardly off the mast before I saw it start to move. Not knowing which way it might go, I backed well out of its way. The movement was slow at first and then, with a sudden jerk, the mast swung upwards in a wide arc so that it now stood upright in the centre of the water. It was still, perhaps for half a minute, before it began to sink down below the surface. I watched it go, foot by foot until the broken end finally disappeared and the water lay still and empty. The ship was gone now, perhaps, no more than a crumbling heap of rotting, water soaked timbers.

The box lay at my feet. I bent down to look at it more closely. It clearly had a lid. I could see the hinges. But I could find neither lock nor any kind of fastening. I pulled hard on the lid. Suddenly, it gave and the box was open.

It was not solid gold. Thin sheets of beaten metal were laid over the surface of some kind of dark wood. Its weight came from a thick lining of lead. The box was not empty. In it lay two shrivelled hands, cut off at the wrists. They were very small, like the hands of a child.

In my mind, I was again seeing the pictures on the walls of the room in the Keefer house, those strange, almost frightening drawings of a child – a child with no hands! What did it mean? Marty had seen those same hands that were now in front of me. Were the drawings of something he had dreamt up in his imagination, or were they drawings of something which he had actually seen?

I was feeling more and more uneasy. That Marty was dead was certain, but how had he died? Marty Keefer was a better swimmer and diver than myself. I remembered those moments in the ship when I had hesitated over taking the box with me. Each time something had happened to persuade me that I must. Had Marty died because the hands had, in some way, prevented him from leaving without them? The thought seemed ridiculous, yet the uncertainty in my mind remained.

But for its covering of gold leaf the box was valueless. I could push it back into the pool (**40**), or should I take it with me (**43**)?

# 39

I woke sometime in the night. It was still dark, but the moon was shining brightly through the windows and onto my pillow. I got up to close the drapes at the bedroom window.

My apartment was on the ground floor and I had a small garden at the back. Both this bedroom and the living room had French windows that opened out onto it.

The night was very still and clear and I paused for a moment, just looking at the garden. Against the darker foliage of a camellia bush, I could see something white. I was trying to decide what it was when it moved and came closer. It stepped from the shadow into the full light of the moon.

At first, I couldn't decide whether it was a boy or a girl. The hair was long and the clothes might have been a dress or some kind of long shirt.

If I hadn't been half asleep, I would have realised that I had used those words before – when describing the drawings of the child on the walls of Marty Keefer's house! I looked at the face. It was pale, with big, dark eyes. I looked at the bare legs and feet. I looked at the hands. There were no hands! The arms ended with the ends of the sleeves and, though I could not see the colour in the moonlight, I could see that the cloth around the wrists was stained with something dark!

I unlocked the French windows and stepped out into the garden. The boy was still there, as clearly as before. I was within two yards of him, when he vanished. There was nothing but lawn around us and no way he could have hidden.

Slowly, I returned to the house, closed the windows, and locked them again. I took two steps on the carpet in my bare feet. The carpet was wet!

I put on all the lights in the apartment. All the doors and windows were closed and, apart from myself, the apartment was empty – yet there were wet footprints in every room!

My mind was slow to accept what I knew had happened. What had happened to Marty had now happened to me. Again, I saw Marty's words, 'I gotta take you back to Coco Plum!' Marty had failed. What chance had I to rid myself of this phantom? I hadn't even got anything to take back!

# 40

The box seemed to sink quite slowly in the water. For a long time, I could see the gold caught in the sunlight that filtered down into the darkness. At last, I could see it no more.

I started my walk back to the Shark River. There, I knew that I would be picked up by the boats which did the regular jungle trips from Flamingo to Everglades City and back. No-one asked any difficult questions. The fact that I had been caught in the hurricane and had been lucky enough to survive it was enough to satisfy anybody curious about my appearance and the fact that I had nothing except the clothes I stood up in.

Flamingo had escaped the worst of the storm, but my first thought was to put as many miles as possible between myself and the Everglades. I arrived back in Wilmington just two days later.

I'd left home with one mystery and come back with half a dozen. I didn't think that I was ever going to be sure of the answers to any of them, but I was determined to get back to a normal life as soon as possible.

I'd arrived home at around noon and had spent the afternoon doing some essential shopping. I arrived back at my apartment just as my help, Mrs Green, who came three times a week, was leaving.

'You have to get out of the shower to answer the telephone?' she enquired.

'When?' I asked.

'Musta been just afore I come. You mighta not been long gone out.'

'No,' I told her. I had had a shower, but the telephone hadn't rung. What made her ask?

'Water,' she said, 'like there was wet footprints all over the carpets – bedrooms, livin' room, most everyplace.'

I could think of no explanation. I had a few indoor plants around the flat which I did water from time to time. That way, I did sometimes spill water; but I couldn't remember watering the plants on my arrival home and, when I checked the pots, they were fairly dry. I ate the meal Mrs Green had left me and went to bed early (**39**).

# 41

Some hundreds of years ago, a child was born in the village of Carmilla. He was both deaf and dumb but, it was found, had miraculous powers of healing in his hands and cured many who were sick. In those days there were many brigands who lived by plundering the villages. A leader of such a band was dreadfully wounded in a fight and was brought by his brother to Carmilla so that the boy might heal him.

The boy tried, but the man died. In rage and grief, the brother first cut off the boy's hands before killing him. The boy's name was Pablo Santos.

The villagers buried the boy, but kept the hands, placing them in a gold box within the tiny church. It was said that now, only by touching the hands, the miracles of healing continued. The story spread and many made pilgrimage to Carmilla, so that the Mission grew in size and became wealthy. So it continued until, one day, pirates came from the coast, stripping the Mission of its treasure and taking also the gold box with the hands of Pablo Santos.

With the hands gone, no-one came to Carmilla and the village became as it was today.

The box was in a small wooden crate at the back of the truck. When the old man finished his story, I asked him to wait while I walked over to the Mission. There, I secretly left the box and returned to the truck.

The old man had got out and was taking his donkey down from the back. He insisted that he was almost home and that he would walk the rest of the way.

'Where is the other?' he asked. 'When we loaded my donkey, I thought that there was a boy already seated on something in the back of the truck.'

I said that his old eyes must be playing him tricks. He could see there was no-one in the truck. I paid him generously for the baskets, thanked him, and turned the truck around to return to Valladolid.

Something made me stop to look back. I could see part of the track beyond the Mission. The old man, who before had let the donkey lead him, was now leading the donkey. The donkey's step showed no limp and was almost sprightly!

I drove on. My story was finished. Perhaps that of Pablo Santos was not. I wanted to think so.

# 42

I made my way back through the saw grass to the point where I had entered it after first seeing the broken mast. Stella Hollis's husband must have had camping gear with him. I saw it, lying near the edge of the island where he must have left it.

I felt deeply sorry for Stella. I felt little for the man. I suspected that he had already killed or attempted to kill in his search for the 'treasure'. I took a ground sheet from his gear and some twine, and used them to wrap up the box. I walked back to Shark River, where I knew I would be picked up by the boats returning from the regular jungle trips to Everglades City.

Flamingo had escaped most of the hurricane, though news of its being on its way had been enough to empty the hotel of some of its rooms. Those visitors had beaten a hasty retreat back to Miami. I was tired, hungry and mentally exhausted. Twenty-four hours in the luxury of a hotel was just what I needed.

After a sound and almost dreamless night's sleep, I woke, thinking that I had been letting my imagination run quite wild – like poor Marty Keefer. As to the strange box, all that I had brought back with me was some harmless religious relic stolen by pirates from a Mexican Mission – thinking it was solid gold. Perhaps some museum might like to have it.

It was after breakfast that I received a polite message from the hotel manager who wished to see me. He looked embarrassed, as if what he was going to say to me would be difficult for him.

'I'm sorry,' he said. 'This must sound quite unfeeling. If it had been only one complaint, I'd have ignored it – but there have been several. It's this boy who has been seen around with you in the hotel. Frankly, the guests find him frightening. I'm sure it's very tragic about his hands, but is there no way it could be made less obvious? I believe they make very good artificial hands these days.'

I now knew what Marty had experienced. I dared not throw the box away. Marty had died in the attempt to rid himself of the phantom child. I saw only one hope left to me (**44**).

# 43

I knew that I had to walk back to Shark River. There I would be picked up by the boats returning from Everglades City to Flamingo after one of the regular tourist jungle trips. I had one problem. I was carrying a large gold box and had nothing to cover it with. The only answer was first to make a call on Gator Jo, the old Indian woman who sold alligator skin purses and wallets to the tourists and whose cabin was on my way.

The cabin was well sheltered by trees and looked as if it had escaped the effects of the hurricane. I hid the box a little way off before going up to the cabin itself. Jo met me at the door. She remembered who I was. I told her that I had been caught in the storm, that I still had a few bits and pieces with me and nothing to carry them in. Could she give me an old sack or something of the kind.

Jo provided a sack and I took it back to where I had hidden the box. As I passed the cabin for the second time, Jo came out to say that she had decided to come with me to Flamingo. She was running short on supplies.

When the boats did arrive, they were fairly full

and Jo and I were separated. We had no more than a few more brief words in Flamingo before we parted.

Flamingo had also escaped the storm, though the news of its coming had been enough to cause some of its visitors to make an early and hasty departure for Miami. That had left the hotel with some empty rooms. I was tired, hungry and mentally exhausted. I decided that I was going to afford myself the luxury of a night in the hotel. After a good meal, I went to bed early and slept soundly until morning.

While I was getting dressed I discovered that the box was missing! There was only one person who could have known that I had the box and I was sure I knew who had taken it – Gator Jo. She could have seen me hide it, or followed me when I went back to put it in the sack.

I knew the box was not valuable and Jo was welcome to have it, but something was wrong. Jo was no thief. She had to have taken it for another reason and I had to go back to find out what that reason was (**45**).

# 44

I knew that the box had come from a Catholic Mission at a place called Carmilla, but I could not find it on any map. I had only one clue. I found the island of Cozumel in Southern Mexico, off the east coast of the Yucatan peninsula. That was the place where Lafitte's ship had anchored and the place from which his men had made the raid on the Mission. If the Mission had once existed then it could be only a few miles inland from the coast.

I flew from Miami to Meridia, the capital of Yucatan, and took a train to the railhead at the small town of Valladolid. That brought me within fifty miles of the coast. To go any further, I would have to hire my own transport. I still had to find the whereabouts of Carmilla and Valladolid seemed as good a place as any to begin to make enquiries. I had plenty of offers to show me the nearby ruins of the Mayan city of Chichén Itzá, but no-one had heard of Carmilla. I decided to try the priest at the local church.

Outside the church was an old man with a donkey. He was selling baskets and pressed me to buy. In English, I said, 'Tell me where to find the Mission of Carmilla and I will buy all of your baskets!'

Answering in Spanish, he said, 'For that, I will take you there. It is by the marshes where I cut reeds for my baskets – but it is a three-day journey for me and my donkey. We are both old. She is a little lame and I am going blind.'

I told him to gather his baskets together and I would return. I did return with an old, open-backed pick-up truck which I'd hired at a ridiculous price. We loaded the donkey and baskets into the back, the old man sitting in the front with me.

The old man could understand a little English, but not speak it. In Spanish, he told me that the Mission, like the town of Carmilla, was but a ruin. After about two hours' drive along no more than a rough cart track he stopped me and pointed. Among tufts of grass and broken rubble I could see pieces of crumbling wall none more than a few feet high.

'That is the Mission,' he said. 'You must have come because of the legend. I had thought that it was long forgotten.'

I asked of what legend he spoke.

'The hands,' he replied, ' – the hands of Pablo Santos.' (**41**)

# 45

Al Baker, one of the Park Rangers was standing outside Jo's cabin when I got there. Al had known my father, having joined the Rangers as a young man when my father was retiring. After the usual enquiries about how I was and what I was doing these days, he asked if I was looking for Jo. I said that I was.

'You just missed her,' he said, 'few minutes back. I looked in to see if she was okay after the hurricane. I ain't sure that she is!'

I asked him what he meant.

'Well,' he said, 'you know Jo – always been a bit of a funny cuss; but I think maybe she's gone a bit odd in the head. When I gets here, she's just comin' out and carryin' somethin' in a sack. Looks like it might be heavy. I asks her if she's comin' back so we might have a word and she comes out with somethin' that don't make a lot o' sense.'

Baker was obviously trying to recall exactly what it was that Jo had said.

'She says she's got a job to finish as was started by her grandfather. She says that her grandfather gave his life to rid himself of an evil spirit, but now that spirit has come back. She says that maybe two people have already died on account of it – and there must be no more. Then she goes off.'

I knew where Jo had gone. I was seeing again the cabin of that sunken ship and the skeleton that still had rags on it and a bracelet of alligator teeth about its wrist.

As a child, I had once called Jo a Seminole Indian.

'Not Seminole!' she had said, indignantly. 'Jo is last of Calusa people – from Mexico, across big water. Can trace ancestors back to great ancient tribes of Mayas and Toltecs.' She had pointed to her wrist and the bracelet of alligator teeth she wore around it. 'Mark of Calusa!' she said. 'Mark of brave warrior. I only woman, but I am last of Calusa and I wear it proudly!'

Jo, like her grandfather, had gone to return the box – perhaps to save my life. Everything to do with the box remained a mystery – except one thing. I could understand Jo, whose Indian name I could not pronounce, had felt this a fitting way to end her life – Jo, last of the Calusa and a 'brave warrior'.

Published by the Press Syndicate of the University of Cambridge
The Pitt Building, Trumpington Street, Cambridge CB2 1RP
32 East 57th Street, New York, NY 10022, USA
10 Stamford Road, Oakleigh, Melbourne 3166, Australia

First published 1985

Printed in Great Britain by the Guernsey Press Co. Ltd, Guernsey

Library of Congress catalogue card number: 84–17511

*British Library cataloguing in publication data*
Sharp, Allen
The Hands of Pablo Santos – (Storytrails)
I. Title    II. Series
823'.914 [J]    PZ7
ISBN 0 521 31706 1

DS

Map by Celia Hart
Cover illustration by David Parkins